THE CONVERGENCE OF GOD'S MANIFESTED SONS

BRINGING FORTH THE FREQUENCIES OF HEAVEN'S ALIGNMENT

APOSTLE DR. MARSHALL MCGEE

THE CONVERGENCE OF GOD'S MANIFESTED SONS

To my Heavenly Father—God, Jesus Christ, and the Holy Ghost—my Creator, Redeemer, and ever-present Helper. You are the Author of my life and the strength behind every word. All glory belongs to You—this offering is Yours.

To my beloved wife, Randi—your quiet strength has been my shelter, your resilience, a flame that never dies. Through valleys and victories, you've stood with me—faithful, fierce, and full of grace. Thank you for believing when the road was unseen, for loving me through every chapter of this journey.

To my precious children—Marshall Jr., Angelica, Immanuel, and Samuel—you are the living proof of God's goodness in my life. Your laughter, your light, your very lives have inspired this work. I pray this legacy reflects the love I carry for each of you.

To my Agape Worship Center Intl. Family—what a joy and sacred honor it has been to serve with you. In worship, in work, in waiting, and in witness—we have built something eternal. Thank you for every prayer, every hand extended, every moment of unity in purpose and love.

To the many spiritual sons and daughters—those who carry a mantle, those who walk with vision, those waiting with holy expectation—may this work illuminate your path as you journey deeper into the dimensions of the Kingdom of God. Creation itself is groaning, waiting to see the full reality of who you are becoming. Arise—take your place.

This book is a testament—of faith, of family, of favor. May it bless you and others as you have so deeply blessed me.

The entire universe is standing on tiptoe, yearning to see the unveiling of God's *glorious* sons and daughters!

ROMANS 8:19 TPT

CONTENTS

FOREWORDS

I first met Apostle Dr. Marshall McGee over thirty years ago, in Kirksville, Missouri. From that divine encounter, a lifelong covenant friendship was born. Relationships are orchestrated by Heaven, undeniable alignments forged for Kingdom purpose. Marshall is one of those rare gifts sent by the Almighty, a true brother in the faith and in the work.

We've journeyed across nations together, stood side by side in sacred moments of ministry, and enjoyed much-needed times of rest and refreshing with our wives during treasured vacations.

I've witnessed firsthand his unwavering passion for truth and deep commitment to advancing God's Kingdom. A prolific preacher and masterful teacher, Marshall carries, with grace and authority, the sound of this present apostolic age. He doesn't just teach it; he embodies it.

In this timely and revelatory book, *The Convergence of God's Manifested Sons*, Marshall unpacks an urgent and eternal subject. With clarity, conviction, and prophetic insight, he speaks to a generation called to mature, manifest, and move in divine sonship.

I urge you to read this work with an open heart and spiritual expectation. This is more than a book. It's a blueprint. Like it has for me and so many others, it will add depth, clarity, and momentum to your journey in God.

Dr. Anthony Earl
City Church Int.
Jeremiah Company
AnthonyEarl.org
Chicago, IL, USA

It is with immense honor and profound gratitude that I pen this foreword for my very good friend, Apostle Marshall McGee. As a fellow citizen in the household of God, I can truly say that I have learned an immeasurable amount from him in countless areas of my life. He is not only a vital part of the Senior Council of the Love & Unity Movement but also a true father in the Body of Christ today.

I am so incredibly glad that Apostle McGee is finally putting into a book the powerful truths he has been teaching for so long. He is a diligent and devoted student of the Word, and the revelation he has received concerning the Scriptures has genuinely changed lives, including my own.

I vividly recall the time Apostle McGee ministered at our house of worship here at Kingdom Family Church in Pomona, California. He delivered a message unlike anything I had ever heard before, on the profound subject of our seated place in the heavens as sons of God from whom we pray. It was a revelation that shifted my understanding and ignited a deeper walk with the Father. When we pray from our seated place with God instead of begging God, we will see great change in our prayer life.

In this transformative book, *The Convergence of God's Manifested Sons,* Apostle McGee delves into crucial kingdom truths, guiding us through the frequencies of God, the manifestation of the sons of God, and, perhaps most importantly, what it truly means to be an ambassador of the Kingdom of God. His insights are not merely theoretical; they are practical, life-altering principles that empower us to live out our divine calling.

Prepare to be challenged, enlightened, and transformed as you delve into the pages of this book. Apostle Marshall McGee is a gift to the Body of Christ, and his teachings are a wellspring of life for all who are hungry for deeper truth and a greater manifestation of God's Kingdom on Earth.

Apostle Eddie Maestas
Love & Unity Movement
Pomona, CA

ENDORSEMENTS

The Convergence of God's Manifested Sons by Apostle Marshall McGee is a refreshing and profoundly helpful contribution to Christian literature. What impressed me most about this work is its commitment to speaking truth in a way that is both accessible and deeply rooted in sound Christian theology.

The book's exploration of frequencies—both earthly and heavenly—and the resulting clash between flesh and spirit provides a remarkably down-to-earth approach to understanding fundamental spiritual dynamics that every believer encounters. One of the most compelling concepts in this book is the discussion of atmospheric shifting and the frequencies of the Kingdom mindset, which our nation and world desperately need to consider.

Apostle McGee's fresh perspective on Kingdom understanding, particularly regarding unseen but manifest frequencies, offers readers a new lens through which to comprehend God's purposes. His ability to make complex spiritual concepts tangible and applicable makes this book an invaluable resource for both personal study and group instruction.

The book brilliantly addresses the critical question of how the body of Christ comes together in unity. McGee's illustration of believers as spokes in a wheel, with Jesus as the hub, demonstrates that when each individual maintains their focus and motivation on Christ, we naturally become united in purpose and direction.

This powerful metaphor reveals how our Christ-centered mindsets automatically align us with God's purposes and with one another. I wholeheartedly recommend *The Convergence of God's Manifested Sons* as a course of study and believe it would greatly benefit from an accompanying workbook to further facilitate learning and application.

Apostle Raymond Mabion
Bethlehem Kingdom Center
Kansas City, Missouri USA

The Convergence of God's Manifested Sons by Dr. Marshall McGee is a book about living a right now, present life, sustained by the power that comes from the convergence and manifestation of God's obedient Kingdom sons. This means that you act, revive, flow, and sustain the territory you have taken, but you no longer try to do it alone, acting like you are the only one. Power and victory in the Kingdom of God comes through individual and corporate obedience—it is all of His sons operating together in the convergence that produces and sustains the high frequencies needed for everyday Kingdom living. This sonship life in only available to the mature sons of the Kingdom of God.

We cannot know how to do this from a low frequency kind of existence, which only steals our energy, hopes, and dreams. The truth is, the Kingdom of God is the only way we are meant to live. Many will never accomplish this, but after eating from the wealth of fruit in this book, you will not be able to continue to live independent of the Kingdom and honestly say you were never told or shown how to do it. *The Convergence of God's Manifested Sons* is a must read and study for every true son, king, and priest in the Kingdom of God.

Apostle Dr Bacer J. Baker, PhD
Host, *Telling It Like It Is: The Kingdom of God Way*
Manteca, CA, USA

In a world hungry for spiritual clarity and Kingdom identity, *The Convergence of God's Manifested Sons* is more than a book; it is a trumpet call to the mature sons of God to rise in truth, power, and alignment. From the opening pages, Apostle McGee delivers revelatory insight that both challenges the status quo and ignites dormant purpose. His teaching on Kingdom frequencies, divine alignment, and the eternal now had us highlighting line after line; not just for knowledge, but because our spirits bore witness to the sound of Heaven within the message.

The chapters: *Sonship Power Awakens Identity*, *Engaging the Eternal Now,* and *A Convergence of Frequencies* are game changers for those who've been sensing there's more to the Christian walk than what religion has shown us. This isn't just inspiration, it's impartation.

This manuscript ministers truth, provokes transformation, and calls readers into action. We recommend this book to five-fold leaders, reformers, intercessors, prophetic voices, and any believer who's tired of waiting on a move of God and is ready to be the move. With the upcoming workbook, we also see this becoming a foundational course of study for discipleship groups, training hubs, and Kingdom-minded leadership teams.

If you're serious about stepping into manifested sonship and shifting atmospheres through divine alignment, don't just read this book, absorb it. Then teach it. Then become it. Amen.

Dr. Kevin Wilson, Prophet - Teacher
Dr. Elonda Wilson, Prophet - Teacher
Words of Wisdom AZ Ministries
Peoria, AZ, USA

As you read the words of Dr. McGee, you will hear the heart of a true Apostolic Father! Rediscover your Kingdom identity through the pages of this urgent narrative. More than a book, more than a teaching of information—there is a cause, and clarion call!

Apostle Dr. Roy Etienne Smith, President
Isaiah University Holy Spirit Seminary
Orlando, FL, USA

In this timely and powerful work, Apostle Dr. Marshall McGee has released a prophetic call for the sons and daughters of God to rise into their given heritage of full Kingdom identity. Rooted in

Romans 8:19 of The Passion Translation, *"The entire universe is standing on tiptoe..."* captures the urgency of Heaven's desire for the children of God to be revealed in divine authority and purpose in the earth.

The Convergence of God's Manifested Sons is a compelling guide for those hungry to be part of an end time unveiling of God's glory through His people, and an important read for those ready to move from potential to manifestations.

Dr. Darryl Udell Sr
Senior Elder
Greater Works Praise & Worship Centre

DR. MCGEE'S KINGDOM TERMINOLOGY

DICTIONARY TERMS & ORIGINAL INTENT DEFINITIONS

Get wisdom, get understanding: forget *it* not; neither decline from the words of my mouth.

PROVERBS 4:5

In this book, we will talk about the gathering and manifestation of the Kingdom of God, the convergence of Sonship, frequency, and divine alignment. This is my assignment from the Lord.

I believe that understanding allows revelation to manifest in our lives. Therefore, my desire is always to gain insight from the Lord, to understand what the scriptures truly say, and to teach with clarity.

As the Bible says, *"Wisdom is the principal thing; therefore get wisdom: and with all thy getting get understanding."* (Proverbs 4:7).

Therefore, we begin with Kingdom terminology and definitions provided specifically for the purpose of ensuring that you have the proper understanding of these terms as used in this book. These dictionary and prophetic definitions are offered to ensure the reader's understanding of specific terms used in this book. *The italicized definitions are spiritually and prophetically defined based on lessons learned from the Holy Spirit.*

ATMOSPHERIC SHIFT
As the people of God tune into the God Frequency, the environment shifts, and divine presence becomes tangible.

CONVERGENCE
When two or more things come together to form a new whole. We can use *convergence* to describe things that are in the process of coming together.[1]

---

1. *Vocabulary.com Dictionary*, s.v. "convergence," accessed

CORPORATE SONSHIP
The gathering moves beyond just worship and teaching; it becomes an activation hub where sons of God arise in their authority.

DISOBEDIENCE
The presence of principles, belief systems, within individuals that are not yet submitted to God's rule.

DIVINE ALIGNMENT
The intent of accurate alignment within God's kingdom through Heavenly influence. The realms of Heaven and Earth operate in accurate synergy, resulting in the influence of Divine, as of God or godly, or His Kingdom intent.
To live in agreement with Father God and Heaven's kingdom agenda, and intent for one's life.

FREQUENCY
The principles and patterns that align with the movement of God.
The rate at which a vibration occurs that constitutes a wave, either in a material

March 27, 2025, https://www.vocabulary.com/dictionary/convergence.

sense, such as sound waves, or an electromagnetic field, such as radio waves or light.[2]

HEAVENLY SUPPLY & PROVISION
As we tune into Heaven's economy, financial breakthroughs, supernatural provisions, and resources manifest.

INSTANTANEOUS MANIFESTATION
Where time and space do not limit the Spirit, what used to take years happens in moments of divine alignment.

MANIFEST[3]
Clearly revealed to the mind or the senses or judgment. synonyms: apparent, evident, patent, plain, resounding, unmistakable, obvious. MANIFEST verb: Provide evidence for; stand as proof of; show by one's behavior, attitude, or external attributes. synonyms: attest, certify, demonstrate, evidence.

---

2. Oxford Languages, s.v. "frequency," accessed February 26, 2025, https://www.google.com/search?q=definition+of+frequency.

3. *Vocabulary.com Dictionary*, s.v. "manifest," accessed March 27, 2025, https://www.vocabulary.com/dictionary/manifest.

PROPHETIC PERCEPTION & REVELATION
People begin to see, hear, and know in the Spirit, accessing divine blueprints and strategies.

SHIFTING ATMOSPHERES
"Spiritual atmospheres are the invisible, heavenly forces that influence the physical world. They can be godly or ungodly, and affect the mood, actions, and even spiritual climate over a person or region."[4]

Display of Kingdom power. The Hebrew word, dabar, implies "creative force." In this context it is spiritual legislation. When a son of God speaks in alignment with Heaven's vibration, all other realms respond to the sound. Timelines shift.
Atmospheres adjust. Also as one carries His presence, wherever it resonates from them the environment shifts or changes and it aligns with the frequency of God that one is carrying. Some of us have entered certain places or rooms and the atmosphere changed or the feeling in the place changed

4. Dawna De Silva, What Are Spiritual Atmospheres? (August 4, 2024), accessed May 2, 2025, https://www.dawnadesilva.com/what-are-spiritual-atmospheres.

because of the One who is so alive
within us.

TRANSRATIONAL
trans·rational: going beyond or surpassing human
reason or the rational.[5]

A knowledge and knowing, a higher, higher learning
—that transcends intellect and formal training.[6]

Knowledge and awareness that is sourced from its
origin, obtained from our seated place in the
heavenlies— cosmic positioning—where we are
literally outside of time and space, seeing and
knowing before it enters the Earth realm.

5. Merriam-Webster.com Dictionary, s.v. "transrational,"
accessed May 31, 2025, https://www.merriam-webster.com/
dictionary/transrational.
6. Brian Orme, speaking on having a knowing and knowledge
in Christ that is higher than higher education—the
transrational/transeducational life, https://www.instagram.com/
reel/DH3oXIOsdAa/?utm_source=ig_web_copy_link.

INTRODUCTION
BY PROPHET, DR. RANDI MCGEE

It is with deep honor, spiritual joy, and unwavering conviction that I write this foreword for *The Convergence of God's Manifested Sons: Bringing Forth the Frequencies of Heaven's Alignment* by my beloved husband, Apostle Dr. Marshall McGee.

After reading the manuscript in its entirety, I can say with full assurance that this is more than just a book—it is a prophetic blueprint and a clarion call for every born-again believer who desires to walk in their true identity as God's Manifested Sons and Daughters in the earth.

Each chapter carries a divine frequency, calibrated to awaken the spirit and realign the reader with Heaven's intent. From the unveiling of Kingdom Reality to the atmospheric shifts through Sonship, the revelation contained in these pages will stir something eternal within you. You will begin to perceive, engage, and manifest the reality of who you are as a son of God—not merely in word, but in power and presence.

The topics Apostle McGee so masterfully unfolds include:

1. The Frequency of Kingdom Reality
2. The Transformation of Our Minds
3. Sonship Power Awakens Identity
4. A Convergence of Frequencies
5. Perceiving As Sons
6. Manifested Sonship
7. Engaging the Eternal Now
8. Kingdom Frequencies Revealed
9. The Atmospheric Shift Through Sonship
10. Foundation of Kingdom Citizenship
11. When We Fully Embrace Our Sonship
12. Answering the Groans of Creation

Having personally witnessed my husband's transformation and the deep revelation he walks in, I can testify that what he writes has been first lived, tested, and proven in his own life. This is not theory —it is spiritual reality.

I believe that as you journey through this book, your spirit will resonate with truth. You will find language for what you've long felt but couldn't articulate. You will encounter frequencies of Heaven that realign your identity, expand your spiritual perception, and release the groaning in your spirit to meet the groaning of creation.

The Convergence of God's Manifested Sons is for every Kingdom heir ready to move from passive belief into active sonship. Prepare to be shifted, aligned, and released.

I am so proud of my husband, Apostle Dr. Marshall McGee, for stewarding this mandate and birthing it into the earth. His obedience and intimacy with the Father are evident in every word.

Let the convergence begin.

A FEW ADDITIONAL NOTES ON DIVINE ALIGNMENT

"…concerned only with foods and drinks, various washings, and fleshly ordinances imposed until the time of *reformation*."

HEBREWS 9:10 NKJV

The Greek word *diorthosis* means "to straighten thoroughly," or "rectification," or can refer to reforming acts or institutions, or restoring something to its original condition. *Diorthosis* also indicates "the act of setting things right or making improvements", which also implies restoration.

The idea is that a reforming or correcting practice, particularly in the realm of Kingdom concepts, aims to **restore things to their original intent,** especially in religious or moral contexts.

Basically, think in terms of restoration or bringing correction of something into right alignment. A clearer definition would be the idea of a skeletal adjustment. When the skeleton is properly adjusted, then the human frame and body operate according to original intent and design.

Another example: when your car is not staying on the road properly, you take it in to get a wheel alignment. When your car is in proper alignment, then your vehicle is restored, and will function at its highest proficiency according to the creator/manufacturer.

Therefore, the context of divine alignment has to do with the intent of accurate alignment, which would equal accurate representation of God's kingdom through heavenly influence. Think of *divine* as of God or godly, or the influence of kingdom intent.

That being so, divine alignment means that the realms of Heaven and Earth operate in accurate synergy, resulting in Heaven and Father God's kingdom agenda having dominion in and over the Earth.

Basically, to be in divine alignment is to live in agreement with Father God and Heaven's intent for one's life. Aligning yourself with the will and purpose of God is divine agreement with Heaven's intent for your life. You are saying, *"Your Kingdom rule come, Your will be done.....in my life."* [1]

Ultimately, divine alignment is a Kingdom corporate mandate to live in harmony and agreement with Father God's purposes, whereby we align our

---

1. See Matthew 6:10.

thoughts, actions, beliefs, and behaviors with the divine intent of the Most High God.

ONE
THE FREQUENCY OF KINGDOM REALITY

*Frequency: The principles and patterns
that align with the movement of God.*

CHAPTER ONE

ONE OF THE THINGS I BEGAN TO ASK THE LORD TO DO
is to give me insight about what the scriptures are
really saying, so that I can have clarity and
understanding. Because when I have clarity and
understanding, then I can teach it to someone else.
I don't just want to know something, I want to
understand it.

It is the Spirit of wisdom who will help us to be able
to look into the true nature of a thing. The Bible
tells us that wisdom is the principal thing. We are to
get wisdom, and in all that we're getting, we will
also get understanding.[1] This is why I want to
make sure that those who listen and learn will hear
according to the meaning of what I am saying, not
what they think I said.

> "Does not wisdom cry out, And
> understanding lift up her voice?...She cries
> out by the gates, at the entry of the city, At
> the entrance of the doors:..."
>
> PROVERBS 8:1, 3

Concerning Wisdom, Proverbs 8:1, 3 says that she
cries out. Our note in the Hebrew context of this
means, *"the perfection of the intellect."* Divine

---

1. Proverbs 4:7

2

intelligence is to walk in wisdom, which is to walk in the perfection of intellect.

If you have been following God any length of time, He has probably asked you to do something that didn't make sense or, to say something that logically is not connecting. It's not that God is illogical. The truth is God is **transrational**; meaning that He is pulling our thought life upwards toward our position in Christ.

That is the perfection of the intellect; it is not just a collection of data so we can repeat stuff. He pulls our thought life up so that the mind of Christ and our mind are in training, so to speak, and there is always synergy (in sync). We will know what to build because we know what's on His mind.

NOTE THAT WISDOM IS CALLING. SHE IS ACTIVE, NOT passive. She releases a frequency, a sound that is coming to the mature sons of God. So, I want to start off with a textbook definition of the word, **frequency**.

Frequency is the rate at which a vibration occurs that constitutes a wave, either in a material sense, such as sound waves, or an electromagnetic field, such as radio waves or light.[2]

ANOTHER WAY TO DEFINE FREQUENCY IS SIMPLY *HOW often something happens.* So as we frequently renew our minds, we grow in wisdom and understanding of the things of God. Understanding is the key that unlocks the manifestation of revelation in our lives.

One more example of this word is *"the principle of how often you do something."* According to medical science, when you have frequency, you have to go to the bathroom a lot. You know that's the truth. So let's get to talking.

I WANT TO SHARE A THEOLOGICAL TRUTH CONCERNING the kingdom of God. We must understand that His Kingdom is not just a future reality, but it is a divine or active divine system that permeates and transforms both visible and invisible realms. I shared this message with a congregation in Texas,

---

2. Oxford Languages, s.v. "frequency," accessed February 26, 2025, https://www.google.com/search?q=definition+of+frequency.

and more recently at a *Love & Unity Convergence*[3], and it bears repeating.

When thinking of the body of Christ, and what God has called and positioned us to do, **we must begin to think both individually and corporately in terms of love and unity**.

We all must understand that our journey as His ecclesia is that of the called out ones, and our journey together is corporate

According to our theological belief system, this means that we must begin to think along the lines of **a Church that is not going to disappear in the clouds.**

Again, we are **not** the Church that plans to disappear into the clouds.[4] God's kingdom operates beyond human *and* satanic systems and enforces the sovereign will of the Father in order to

----

3. Love & Unity is a movement that works to build apostolic and prophetic foundations and teams across regions, states, and countries. To find out more about this moment, visit www.love-unity.org.

4. The expression, "We are not a church that plans to disappear into the clouds" is something I heard from Dr SY (Sagie) Govender, *Accurate Building Concepts Ministries*, Republic of South Africa. abcministries.co.za.

bring His eternal purposes into every realm. Both in *and* outside of the earth.

We are the Church that is appearing! We are bringing forth the manifestation of the King and His kingdom, His righteousness and His peace and judgment into the earth realm. I say that, because to understand the kingdom of God, we must understand that **we live in multiple realms at the same time.**

WE MUST UNDERSTAND THAT WE LIVE IN MULTIPLE REALMS AT THE SAME TIME.

GOD'S KINGDOM DOES NOT JUST OPERATE EXTERNALLY. It must be established within the hearts of people. That's one of the greatest hindrances to the Kingdom message, and why people resist the message when they hear it.

They have **internally built systems of wrong belief**, coming from wrong indoctrination that has developed deep-rooted opinions and traditions **that they hold onto**. Their beliefs, thoughts, opinions, and lives are not yet fully submitted to God's rule.

People that resist the Kingdom message are programmed to say things like, *"I'm loyal to the denomination. I'm loyal to the Pope...I'm loyal to all these things."* These are the words that activate worldly belief systems inside of people, causing **an automatic resistance** to believe the truth whenever the message of the Kingdom is taught. This aligns with what Jesus said in Luke's gospel:

> *Neither shall they say, Lo here! or, lo there! for behold, the kingdom of God is within you.*

LUKE 17:21

He said that the kingdom of God is within you. The God's kingdom within us operates beyond human and even satanic systems. You and I, as Kingdom ambassadors, are able to enforce the Sovereign Will of God that is in our lives.

More specifically, we do this **within our hearts** in every dimension of life, both naturally and spiritually.

> *"...the kingdom of God is within you."*

YOU HAVE TO KNOW THAT THE KINGDOM IS NOT something that's *"way out there"*. Again, the kingdom of God **is within you,** ***and it operates through us*** (that's you and me). However, while many people have *heard* about the kingdom, **most people don't ever see it manifest in their lives.**

This is an issue that must be reversed.

Here's the point. **If God the Father through the Holy Spirit does not reveal the Kingdom to you, then you'll never be able to see how to live in the reality of it.** The Lord taught me that the Kingdom is preached a lot *because* **it is in you.**

AND THAT IS WHY ONE OF THE MANDATES ON MY LIFE IS to teach God's people the reality of both Kingdom life and Kingdom living.

TWO
THE TRANSFORMATION OF OUR MINDS

Transformation: the Kingdom process that must take place first in the hearts of the sons, so that it can manifest in the world around us.

And be not conformed to this world: but be ye transformed by the renewing of your mind, that ye may prove what is that good, and acceptable, and perfect, will of God.

ROMANS 12:2

ONE OF THE GREATEST HINDRANCES TO THE FULL manifestation of the Kingdom is the presence of internal belief systems that are not yet fully submitted to God's rule. Unless the internal structure of one's belief system changes, they will not be able to fully access what our God is doing, and how He is now moving within the earth realm through a yielded people.

Another major hindrance to the full manifestation of the Kingdom in our lives is **disobedience.**

> **Disobedience** is the presence of principles or belief systems within individuals that are not yet submitted to God's rule.[1]

Beliefs that we hold on to are beliefs that are not submitted to the authority of the King. Some people resist the message of the Kingdom because

---

1. See Dr. McGee's Kingdom Terminology.

of deeply ingrained religious traditions within their hearts.

We mentioned earlier that the Kingdom must be established *within* the hearts of people. Instead of giving their loyalty to the Father and King, it is fixed toward their denomination.

> *"This people draweth nigh unto me with their mouth, and honoureth me with their lips; but their heart is far from me."*
>
> MATTHEW 15:8 KJV

What does this mean? It means that transformation must first take place in our hearts before it can manifest in the world around us. Another way to say it is that *our frequency must transform from those deeply ingrained religious traditions and unsubmitted internal belief systems to Heaven's belief system.*

WE MUST STOP BEING CONFORMED TO THE BELIEFS OF this world, and be transformed by the renewing of our minds.[2] This is what will *change our frequency.*

---

2. Romans 12:2

"Wisdom is the principal thing; therefore get wisdom: and with all thy getting get understanding."

PROVERBS 4:7

Again, the Kingdom of God is not just a future reality, but an active, divine system that transforms both the visible and invisible realms. **When we speak of frequency in a spiritual sense, we are referring to the principles and patterns that align with the movement of God.** It is through us, the sons of God, that the Kingdom operates beyond human and satanic systems, enforcing the sovereign will of God in every dimension.

THE KINGDOM COMES BY REVELATION. SO EVEN IF YOU have heard preaching, teaching, and more teaching, you'd better learn how to open your spirit, so that the revelation can truly get inside of you. You will have to give up some old beliefs so that the revelation can come, and so that you can learn how to live out of the reality of what you heard. Because **God's kingdom is a real place that we live in.**

Unless the internal structure of our belief system changes, we will not be able to fully access what our God is doing and how He is now moving within the earth realm through a yielded people. I call it *the reality of Kingdom life and Kingdom living*.

**God's Kingdom Is
A Real Place
That We Live In.**

ARE YOU UP FOR THE TRANSITION FROM WHAT USED TO be and once was to what is NOW?

THREE
SONSHIP POWER AWAKENS IDENTITY

Sonship: "The convergence of power that awakens our Kingdom identity." ~ Nancy Cohen

JESUS, THE SON OF GOD, BECAME THE SON OF MAN
so that the sons of men could become the sons of
God. This is a powerful summary of Christ's
redemptive purpose. Jesus, the Son of God
became the Son of Man, **so that the sons of men
can become the sons of God.**[1]

**Jesus The Son Of God
Became The Son Of Man
So That The Sons Of Men
Could Become
The Sons Of God.**

---

1. Often quoted by modern-day ministers, in fact, I heard it
first from Nancy Cohen, this saying is historically attributed to
St. Athanasius: *"Jesus the Son of God became the Son of Man,
so that the sons of men might become sons of God."* While
widely cited in contemporary theology, this phrasing is a
paraphrase rather than a direct quote from the original Greek. It
summarizes a central theological assertion found in *On the
Incarnation*, §54. The actual line is closer to: **Αὐτὸς γὰρ
ἐνηνθρώπησεν, ἵνα ἡμεῖς θεοποιηθῶμεν**—"He became man
that we might be made god." See St. Athanasius, *On the
Incarnation*, trans. and ed. John Behr (Yonkers, NY: St.
Vladimir's Seminary Press, 2011), 107; also trans. Penelope
Lawson (Crestwood, NY: St. Vladimir's Seminary Press,
1996), 54.

As the Son of Man, Jesus fully identified with humanity so that through His sacrifice and resurrection, we could be transformed, restored to sonship with the Father. The greatest awakening is not external—it is the awakening of sonship identity, the knowledge of which unlocks our sonship authority. John's gospel says:

"But as many as received him, to them gave he power to become the sons of God, even to them that believe on his name..."

JOHN 1:12

The scripture says He gave the right or the power or the authority to become sons of God to as many as receive Him. We are not just believers; we are **sons with power and authority**. That means that:

- We do not ask for dominion; we walk in it because it was given to us.
- The world is not against us; it is actually waiting for us to take our place.

The book of Romans tells us that the sons of God are those who are led by His Spirit.

"For as many as are led by the Spirit of God, these are the sons of God. For you did

not receive the spirit of bondage again to fear, but you received the Spirit of adoption, by whom we cry out, 'Abba, Father.' The Spirit Himself bears witness with our spirit that we are children of God, and if children, then heirs—heirs of God and joint heirs with Christ, if indeed we suffer with Him, *that we may also be glorified together."*

ROMANS 8 14-17 NKJV

This passage in Romans identifies God's sons as His *huios*, His mature sons. It is the mature sons who walk in intimacy with the Father and operate from a place of divine alignment—a portal, a doorway if you will—is opened where divine Kingdom realities override earthly limitations.

Truly there are sons that have this kind of intimacy with the Father, **yet *intimacy with Father* is also something that a number of ministry leaders lack.** And so when the doorway opens, they can't step in. Now, if you're really going to come into intimacy, you have just got to disrobe the flesh. *I will say what I said again.* To truly come into intimacy with Father, we must all disrobe or separate from our flesh and carnal desires.

Here's the point. You've got to take your flesh off. You've got to just *lose your Earth system-bound* *mind* if you're going to step into the river of the move of the Spirit of God.

Let me make it simple. When we all do that, then when the sons of God gather in unity, we become a collective force that releases God vibrations, transforming the atmosphere, altering the course of nations, and manifesting Heaven's reality on Earth.

HERE'S THE PROBLEM. PEOPLE ARE TRYING TO COME into intimacy with a mixture. We have problems in the prophetic because people want to come into corporate gatherings with a mix of this, that, and other things that do not align with the mind of the Spirit. This is hypocrisy, and it will no longer be tolerated among the leaders of God's people.

> *"Woe to those who polish the outside of the cup while the inside is filthy. Woe to the whitewashed tombs—beautiful on the outside, but full of dead men's bones."*
>
> MATTHEW 23:27 [AUTHOR'S PARAPHRASE]

When our hearts are truly renewed, we won't need the choir robes, the bishop's rings, or the ridiculous hats to validate us. The glory of God will be our covering. The purity of our walk will be our authority. I heard my spiritual father, Dr. Anthony Earl, say this:

> "This will not be a season for showmanship. It is a time for substance. Authenticity must replace performance. Doctrine must match lifestyle. Costumes are for clowns. Your credibility doesn't come from your robes, rings, or titles—it comes from your consecrated life. It is not the outer garment that God is inspecting; it is the condition of the inner man."
>
> ~ Apostle Dr. Anthony Earl

I'LL SAY IT AGAIN SO YOU CAN GET THIS DOWN WITHIN your spirit. Our greatest awakening is not external or outward—**it must come from our awakening of Sonship identity! This is the knowledge which unlocks our authority.** This is what happens when the mature sons of God come together and gather outside of the traditions of men and even denominational protocols, and therefore submit to the way that the Father wants things done right here in the Earth.

And that is why our Kingdom gatherings *shall be* the converging place where the glory frequency is dominant. So that the portal does open, and the **divine realities of God's kingdom do override earthly limitations in His sons.**

FOUR
A CONVERGENCE OF FREQUENCIES

Convergence: When the sons of God
gather in unity, they release divine
vibrations that shift atmospheres and alter
the course of nations.

CHAPTER FOUR

Acts 2:1-4 describes the day of Pentecost as a demonstration of corporate alignment. The upper room gathering of 120 people was a convergence —an event where unity in the Spirit caused the Holy Spirit to manifest tangibly. It was so powerful that in the aftermath, they went out and shifted the atmosphere everywhere they went.

This event was a Kingdom gathering, called by God Himself to create a convergence of frequencies to be amplified by the Holy Spirit. Simply put,

---

Convergence Is When Two Or More Things Come Together To Form A New Whole.

---

*The term convergence can also be used to describe **things that are in the process of coming together.***[1] So, when you think in terms of a convergence, think about how different streams come together. Can you see why Kingdom gatherings are not merely an assembly of believers

---

1. *Vocabulary.com Dictionary*, s.v. "convergence," accessed March 27, 2025, https://www.vocabulary.com/dictionary/convergence.

or a Christian conference? A convergence is a *spiritual call to come together*, it is where sons of God begin to align with the God frequency—the frequency of Heaven. The purpose is so that Heaven can bring forth the Kingdom realities within us into the Earth realm.

SOMETHING TRULY POWERFUL HAPPENS WHEN GOD'S sons converge in unity. Our alignment amplifies the manifestation of Father's glory, and when this thing begins to happen, an exchange takes place. We see the Kingdom truly manifesting according to His design. When there's a true convergence, things begin to and forever will explode in the Earth, because the Spirit of God begins to overwhelm us.

Behold, how good and how pleasant it is for brethren to dwell together in unity!

PSALM 133:1

There is so much to unpack in that scripture. Do you know how powerful it is when believers come together in unity? To understand what is being released, we first must know that every person on earth carries a spiritual frequency. But the highest frequencies available to humanity are those that vibrate within the true sons of God.

The Highest Governing Frequency In All Creation Is The Love Of God In And Through His Christ That Manifests Through The Sons Of God.

HERE'S WHAT YOU NEED TO UNDERSTAND. IN THE BIBLE in just about every instance where unity is called for, it is referring to man's relationship with Jesus, *NOT* with other men. That's right.

The concept of Unity in the Hebraic context is about each individual person's union with Jesus. Unity flows from man to Jesus, **not from believer to believer**. Whatever unity there is to be between men must flow through The Lord Jesus Christ.

Think of The Lord Jesus as being like the hub of a spoked wheel.

- He is the central point to which all believers are connected. Note that the spokes of a hubbed wheel *aren't* connected with each other.
- The spokes are connected to the "hub."

Any unity that exists between the spokes is because they are connected to the hub, or Jesus.

NOTE THAT WE ALL HAVE DIFFERENCES. AND SOMETIMES those differences create tensions because we are all so different. We must think about Unity in the context of being *"the place where God commands The Blessing!!!"* We therefore also must understand that it is our differences that Father God wants to use to bring us to a place called **Corporate Dominion**.

The Greek word for *dominion* is **kratos,** which is also defined as strength, power; or a mighty deed.

- The fact is we all have the Holy Ghost; yet some of us have a different measure of grace.
- Some have a different operation of the Spirit to work under.

PSALM 133:3 SAYS THAT UNITY IS LIKE THE DEW OF Hermon on the mountains of Zion: the place where God commands **The Blessing**. This is prophetic language the conveys a message. Mount Hermon in one meaning meant *"Snowy Mountain."*

- This is one of the highest places geographically. A high mountain as well.
- The prophetic picture is that of the dew/moisture from the tops of the mountain would flow down into the place of Mt Zion.
- As a result of the refreshing, fruitfulness was produced.
- And it is there in the place of fruitfulness that God commands The Blessing.

If we can get over ourselves and come into the Place called Unity, it is **There That God Will Command The Blessings And Life Forever More.** Hear the Word of the Lord!!! **"Unity"** is the place where God commands **The Blessing.** *In unity* we will see the power of corporate vision. According to Webster's dictionary:

> **Command** means to order or charge with authority, control, exercise supreme authority over.

I BELIEVE THAT THIS IS THE PLACE WHERE THE CHURCH can enter into what I call, *"Corporate Dominion."* This is where we become a people so in love with Him and one another—believers becoming so "one" that whatever we decide to do....whatever we want to accomplish...it is done! Can you imagine us being that people? This can only come out of a community of people who have the same wants and desires, the same heartbeat.[2]

HOW DOES CONVERGENCE HAPPEN TODAY? WHAT does it look like? We saw it in Acts 2. First, there must be a deep internal transformation where our thoughts, desires, and principles begin to align with His will. The more we learn to yield to His rule in our hearts, the more His kingdom will be demonstrated through our lives. Everybody brings their gift. Everybody brings their anointing, and when we come together, there's a release of divine vibrations that shifts the atmosphere. That's when we begin to ultimately affect the world around us.

The Church must shift from fear to glory. Many believers have been conditioned to expect fear, gloom, and doom, unintentionally manifesting the frequency of destruction. When we shift our corporate expectation to the glory of God, we begin to see the greater works of Jesus manifesting.

---

2. Genesis 11:1-9 talks about this kind of oneness of language, vocabulary, and vision. But the people were not interested in pursuing oneness to the glory of God, so they ended up with Babel, a confused mixture.

A Kingdom Gathering should be a place where the glory frequency is dominant—a portal, a doorway if you will, where divine realities override earthly limitations. That's what happens when the sons of God gather—*moving out of our traditions of men and denominational protocol*—to submit **to the way Father wants things done in the earth**. This is the formation of unity.

We, the sons of God, release His divine vibrations to shift atmospheres and alter the course of nations. This is how Heaven's reality is manifested in the Earth realm. Which is why it is entirely possible for you to experience a breakthrough while you're reading this book.

———

NOW, LET ME SAY THIS BEFORE I GET TOO FAR. IN OUR circles, you hear many of us say, *"I believe God, I believe God"* a lot. But most people among us *don't really know how* to believe God! May I give you a key here? Some prophetic insight, really.

When one has developed an intimate relationship with Father, Son, and Spirit; you don't try to believe! Hear Me! When you have an intimate relationship with Him, *you don't try* to believe. No, instead you just **operate from** the relationship.

May I suggest then, if you truly know in your heart that you don't have a real intimate relationship with Him, remember what is written in John's gospel. Jesus said He would send **another Comforter** to lead and guide us into all truth.

Note that the Person of the Holy Spirit is the Spirit of Truth, and if there's something that you don't understand, or don't know how to do to be in a relationship with Him, you can ask the Holy Spirit to help you. He will help you to develop a true and intimate relationship with the Lord Jesus Christ. Just ask Him.

The same is true in corporate gatherings. When you go to a meeting, you don't go to merely be an observer. You go both to give *and to r*eceive. That's an example of intimacy. The Holy Ghost is the Helper *and* He will help and show you what to do.

So, as you continue to read, I exhort you to position (open and give entrance to) your heart to receive from a Higher frequency.

FIVE
PERCEIVING AS SONS

Perceiving: Moving in the working knowledge of sonship identity to the degree that we only act upon Father's words and actions.

"Then Jesus answered and said to them, 'Most assuredly, I say to you, the Son can do nothing of Himself, but what He sees the Father do; for whatever He does, the Son also does in like manner.'"

JOHN 5:19

WE MUST UNDERSTAND THAT SEEING IN THE SPIRIT IS not just about having visions—it is about perceiving, knowing, and experiencing the reality of the Kingdom. We can access anything that is relevant because we have learned to live from the eternal realm, now. Therefore we understand that we can see into the future.

Note this case study from John 5:19. When Jesus said, *"I only do what I see the Father do,"* we get to see that He was constantly *connected to the realm of heaven.*[1] In the same way, He has also given us the opportunity to be connected.

So, What Realm Are You Connected To? Are you connected to the earthly realm most of the time, and occasionally a little bit of Heaven? Or do you constantly live in two realms? Can you be

_____

1. Mike Parsons, "Connecting to the Realm of Heaven," *Freedom ARC* (blog), September 23, 2011, https://freedomarc. wordpress.com/2011/09/23/connecting-to-the-realm-of-heaven/

connected to both every minute, every fraction of a second, of every day?

According to Healthline,[2] the average teen/adult blinks 15 to 20 times per minute. There are 1,440 minutes in a day, so you likely blink about 21,600 times per day. That means, while you're awake, you probably blink:

- 900 – 1,200 times an hour
- 14,400 – 19,200 times a day
- 100,800 – 134,400 times a week
- Between 5.2 and 7.1 million times a year

Given how many times the average person blinks per minute, with each blink lasting between 0.1 and 0.4 seconds, this makes up about 10 percent of the time you're awake.

When you think in spiritual terms, this "blinks us" in and out of that spiritual realm like a nanosecond—and a nanosecond is one billionth of a second.

---

2. Scott Frothingham, "How Many Times Do You Blink a Day?," *Healthline,* February 3, 2023, https://www.healthline.-com/health/how-many-times-do-you-blink-a-day

That's a bit hard to get hold of, but the reality is we are constantly connected to the spiritual realm–or we can be. So what are you seeing? Whose voice are you resonating with?

In a Kingdom Gathering, we are intentionally activating people through the *ministry of impartation* to be trained to engage the unseen realm, activating their spiritual senses. This means that worship, teaching, and prophetic encounters should *move beyond* information and into impartation, so people don't just hear about God's Kingdom, but experience it firsthand.

Thinking Non-Locally Brings Instant Manifestation

In a Kingdom Gathering, we are not gathering locally—we are gathering in the Spirit with heavenly hosts, saints, and divine beings. When we step into this reality, manifestation becomes immediate because we are not bound by earthly time.

Healing, miracles, and divine downloads happen in an instant when we shift from local, linear thinking to eternal, non-linear engagement.[3]

---

3. Paraphrase from a teaching by Prophet Darnell Craig, Heart of God Ministries, International. It not the total word, but I just wanted to give him some credit.

SIX

MANIFESTED SONSHIP

Manifest: The release of divine vibrations that shift atmospheres and alter the course of nations.

"...and raised *us* up together, and made *us* sit together in the heavenly *places* in Christ Jesus."

EPHESIANS 2:6

IN KINGDOM GATHERINGS, WE MUST ENGAGE BEYOND the intellect or our studies and knowledge, and step into the realm of experience, where our spirit leads, and our soul follows the direction of the Holy Spirit. The church has often limited itself by linear thinking (step-by-step processes), instead of functioning from heavenly places where everything is already complete. Manifestation happens when we engage spiritually.

To actually function from the seated place, we must move from *merely believing* in heavenly places. Belief is not enough to manifest what is already established in the Spirit. This is the truth awakening within us now.

> For the earnest expectation of the creation eagerly waits for the revealing of the sons of God.

ROMANS 8:19

The greatest awakening is not an external event. Our great awakening is the perceived reality of our sonship identity, and the actions we perform from this revelation.

- We are not just believers; we are sons with authority.
- We do not ask for dominion. We walk in it because it was given to us.
- The world is not against us; it is actually waiting for us to take our place.

WE CARRY GOD'S DNA—WE ARE NOT COPIES, WE ARE direct extensions of His nature. Reality bends to identity, because our DNA carries the blueprint for restoration. The sons of God are the only beings in creation that carry God's spiritual Genetic Code. This means we don't just reflect light—*we are light.*

Romans 8:19 declares that Creation is waiting for the revealing of the sons. It is waiting for the Manifest Sons of God to Govern. This tells us that:

Creation is not in rebellion. It is waiting for the leadership of those who carry the Father's DNA.

Creation is not groaning for more churches, but for sons to take their place.

- Sons restore what Adam lost.
- Sons rule through intimacy, not control.

- Sons bring Kingdom order to business, government, and culture.

When the sons speak, we release the creative power of God, shifting atmospheres and transforming realities. Jesus demonstrated this when He spoke to storms, healed the sick, and multiplied resources.

He wasn't just performing miracles—He was governing creation as a Son. This is our design, our spiritual blueprint. Sons don't pray for permission—we operate in delegated authority.

> **"SONSHIP is a fundamental principle of representation. A son never lives for himself. A son is only on the earth to represent his Father. In the son the Father is glorified, and whatever the son does, he only does it when he hears his Father say it, or he sees his Father do it. That's the principle of SONSHIP."**

Thamo Naidoo, Presiding Apostle
Senior Elder, Gate Ministries,
Sandton, South Africa

THE KINGDOM OF GOD IS NOT ADVANCED BY RELIGIOUS effort, but by sons manifesting the Father's will on Earth. Creation was designed to serve the sons of God, not the other way around.

The world around you mirrors the level of awareness you carry. The moment you awaken to your authority, everything begins to align.

Reality bends to identity.

If we think like slaves, creation resists us. But when we walk in sonship, manifestation happens as everything aligns with the will of God.

SEVEN
ENGAGING THE ETERNAL NOW

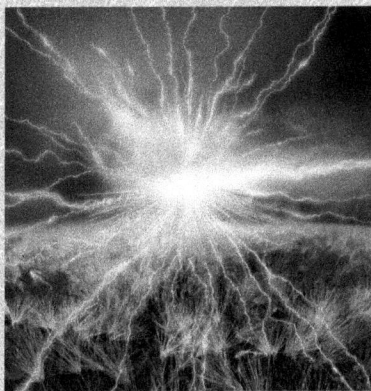

Engage: When the sons of God come together to be about their Father's business, divine vibrations release on assignment to shift atmospheres and manifest Kingdom realities.

"All things were created through Him and for Him. And He is before all things, and in Him, all things hold together."

COLOSSIANS 1:16-17

SONS OF GOD ARE NOT REACTIONARY; WE ARE governors of the seen and unseen realms. As we shift from thinking as servants to thinking as sons, we stop chasing solutions and start commanding them.

Manifestation comes through awareness, meaning that you don't need more power—you need more awareness of who you already are. The moment you recognize that creation is coded to respond to you, you stop living in limitation. Remember, the world is not waiting on another revival—it is waiting on the sons to manifest.

Governing through sonship means ruling and stewarding the earth as mature sons and daughters of God, operating from identity, not striving. It's about bringing Heaven's order into every sphere of society through wisdom, authority, and love.

We are co-heirs with Christ, meaning everything He governs, we govern with Him. Jesus did not perform miracles just for the sake of signs—He governed creation as a Son. That's because He didn't come to start a religion. Jesus came to restore Sonship.

> "But as many as received Him, to them He gave the right to become children of God, to those who believe in His name:..."

JOHN 1:12

True Authority Flows From Sonship, Not Performance.

- Jesus ruled by relationship with the Father (John 5:19)
- Jesus said, I only do what I see my Father doing.
- He exercised dominion—over nature, sickness, and death, healing the sick and raising the dead—again, without striving.
- He operated in love, not control—He governed with supernatural authority.
- He spoke to storms and calmed them.
- He multiplied resources through divine authority.

Everything Jesus did revealed how sons govern—by oneness with the Father. This is our spiritual blueprint. Religious people strive for power, but God's sons walk in inheritance.

**Sons of God do not ask for permission.
Sons of God operate in delegated authority.
Sons of God command solutions.**

Living from the Eternal Now is an interesting and profound reality. It is about stepping out of time-based limitations. Think of **now** as, *"Now,* because I believe, everything in the eternal realm is always NOW!"* Understand that from *there (Heaven's seat),* we serve in a limitless borderless Kingdom. ***There*** we live from an elevated, ascended perspective of God's finished redemption work through Christ.

- As we learn to live *from* the eternal now, we don't pray for healing. We release it.
- We don't chase purpose. We reveal it through our lives.
- Isaiah 9:6 declares that of His government there is no end, and there is never-ending increase.
- He raised us up together with Himself, and made us sit in heavenly places with Christ Jesus, therefore *we are seated* in heavenly places (Ephesians 2:6).

Living from the Eternal Now means:

- You are governed by eternity, not circumstance.
- You live in sync with Heaven, not the pressures of culture.
- You draw from a finished reality, not a future hope.

You no longer just wait for God to move—you realize He's already moved, and you move with Him.

- Living from the Eternal Now is union-consciousness.

Acts 17:28. *In Him we live, move, and have our being.* He said to me once, "Flip it around." Then He simply said, and I believe He's saying it to all of us, "It's in you. That's you. In you, I live, I move, and I have my being." He's in us. See Him living moving and having His very essence and nature living through your life.

- Time doesn't dictate your life—Heaven does.
- In this awareness, you engage in instant access to the Father.

- Spirit-led timing, where Kairos moments override Chronos time.
- Prophetic flow, where future realities can be drawn into the present by faith.

THE MORE WE CAN TOUCH THESE DIMENSIONAL REALMS, the more will be able to literally operate from the eternal...*now*. We are seated in Christ, next to the Father, therefore there are no limitations. Part of the dynamic with this seating—I call it cosmic positioning—is that we are **literally outside of time and space.**[1]

> **Note:** Our God exists outside of time. Hear me. He is *I AM*, *not* I was or I will be. He is *I AM*. The eternal now is the place where all the promises of God are, Yes and Amen (1 Corinthians 1:20).

Therefore, as believers we stop struggling, hoping for breakthrough. We entered into this place as our present reality. According to the eleventh chapter of Hebrews, **faith is now**, so we enter into the *Now Faith* room. You must touch this eternal realm. Let's just call it NOW for now.

---

1. I first heard this phrase, "cosmic positioning" used by Brian Orme.

John 19:30. *It is finished.*

Everything that is needed: identity, access, authority, and inheritance is already completed.

Hebrews 4:3. *His works were finished from the foundation of the world.*

Jesus did not say the Kingdom is coming. He said *the Kingdom is at hand*.

Mark 1:15. *"Is here" implies present. Touchable. Reachable.*

We are not waiting for Heaven. We are to live as if it is already here, because it is available to us **NOW.**

The Blueprint for Kingdom Governance

A. **Know Your Identity**

You are not a servant trying to earn favor. You are a son with full access (Galatians 4:6-7).

B. **Govern Through Relationship, Not Performance**

Jesus ruled by hearing the Father, not by religious works.

Sons operate from intimacy, not striving.

Sons don't control people—they transform culture.

True governance is about restoring, not manipulating.

C. Govern Through Ruling and Reigning

Religion strives, and has taught us to live for approval. It teaches us to identity with certain denominational thinking and reasoning. We govern as sons.

HEAR ME! IN KINGDOM REALITY WE UNDERSTAND THAT we are here to live from our Sonship. This is the approval given to us.

Therefore we live from victory **because of Jesus' resurrection**, and also because we understand our seated position in Him.

EIGHT

KINGDOM FREQUENCIES REVEALED

"The Son is the dazzling radiance of God's splendor, the exact expression of God's true nature—his mirror image! He holds the universe together and expands it by the mighty power of his spoken word. He accomplished for us the complete cleansing of sins and then took his seat on the highest throne at the right hand of the majestic One."

HEBREWS 1:3 TPT

GOD'S KINGDOM IS LIMITLESS. IT OPERATES BEYOND the constraints of time—which is why we do not need more power. We need greater awareness of who we already are. The moment we recognize that creation is coded to respond to us, we stop living in limitation.

Remember, Jesus said, *"I only do what I see My Father do,"* meaning, that the more we engage in spiritual perception, the more we live from the eternal now, rather than being bound by time. For the kingdom of God to manifest fully, there must be a deep internal transformation within each of us, where our thoughts, desires, and principles align with His will. The more we yield, the more the Kingdom is demonstrated through us, affecting everything around us.

A KINGDOM GATHERING SHOULD BE A PLACE WHERE THE glory frequency dominates—a portal where divine realities override earthly limitations. Many believers have been conditioned to expect fear, doom, and destruction, unintentionally manifesting the frequency of lack.

However, when we shift our corporate expectation to the glory of God, we intentionally manifest the frequencies of God's kingdom. And that's when we begin to see greater works manifest.

Divine alignment is only manifested from the convergence of sonship; occurring when the sons of God gather together in the Spirit, think from the eternal realm, and learn to release only what the Father says and does. As we learn to think from the eternal realm, we will see the Kingdom of God established in power upon the earth.

You are called in this time to step into your full identity, speak with authority, and align the world around you with the original blueprint of Heaven. We've said it before: creation will not shift until we do. The Kingdom is not coming—it is here, within us.

The only thing missing is manifested sons who know who they are.

NINE

THE ATMOSPHERIC SHIFT THROUGH SONSHIP

HOW THIS MANIFESTS IN A KINGDOM GATHERING

"And the earth was without form, and void; and darkness *was* upon the face of the deep. And the Spirit of God moved upon the face of the waters."

GENESIS 1:2 KJV

BY NOW YOU UNDERSTAND THAT WHEN GOD'S SONS gather in unity, we become a collective force that releases the God vibrations that shift atmospheres. We alternate the course of nations because we manifest Heaven's reality in the Earth realm. I believe every region we occupy needs to be altered by the reality of Heaven. So, how does this connect to Kingdom Gathering and manifestation?

Each one of us carries a spiritual frequency. When we come together as believers who connect with each other in unity, we create a wonderful harmony in the Spirit that causes a release of the God frequency that we each carry within. Working from the inside, our unity produces a powerful manifestation of the glory of God within our midst.

To say it differently, I believe that when we all come together in a corporate Kingdom Gathering, where everyone is bringing their part, what happens is that we start looking like Jesus. The more we start looking like Him, and the greater His corporate body in this earth realm becomes, is when the Jesus things begin to manifest.

Have you ever been in a worship service when the man or woman of God moves by the Spirit to bring everyone into alignment with Him? If you have experienced this, did you sense the manifestation of God's glory? He is such a tangible Presence that when He reveals Himself the entire atmosphere of the room is charged. That frequency change comes from unity. It doesn't leave, it only grows stronger in this kind of atmosphere because everybody carries something in the Spirit.

In a Kingdom gathering, as our joint frequencies begin to shift into alignment is also when we begin to resonate with Heaven. In corporate sonship, we attract and manifest divine supply, healing and breakthrough from the unseen realm. It comes into the material world.

Acts 2:1 tells us that when the day of Pentecost fully came, there was a demonstration of corporate alignment. And that's when the unity of the Spirit caused a manifestation of the Holy Spirit in a visible and tangible way. That's what we're looking for! We're looking for visible manifestations of the Spirit of God, **not the flesh**.

I believe there are false manifestations that look like, and act like—**but just ain't** the real Spirit of

God. We know this is true, because lives don't get transformed. Yes. Folks fall on the floor, but nothing changes when they get up.

That ain't us! So we're looking for the Acts 2 demonstration, the one that happens because of corporate alignment. The one that happens because the mature sons of God have gathered together, so there must be a full manifestation.

> "For the earnest expectation of the creation eagerly waits for the revealing of the sons of God."

> ROMANS 8:19

What a powerful end-time ministry the manifest sons of God have been given. God loves the whole cosmos, but it is waiting for us to mature as sons ([that is the huios in Greek, which is the mature son, not a child). He has chosen us, and given us the responsibility to exercise dominion. He is not going to do this for us.

We know that the Bible says that creation is waiting for the manifestation of the sons of God, but do we also know that manifestation requires there be a divine alignment? We've got to come into alignment. Not like, *"Oh, I like that message."* No, we must come into alignment in the spirit, because Jesus is the one that sets the course.

God is looking for sons who know the truth, the full reality of who our Father is; sons who see Him as He truly is—see ourselves as we truly are, created in His image. Meaning that when we line up with Him, and when we come together, we should automatically fall into alignment. Do you want to see manifestations of power?

Then get in alignment.

Can you remember the last place you were and you didn't see anything? Well, remember that *you were there*.

So get in alignment.

TEN

FOUNDATION OF KINGDOM CITIZENSHIP

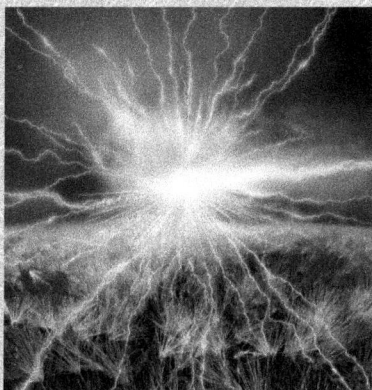

"All things were created through Him and for Him. And He is before all things, and in Him, all things hold together."

COLOSSIANS 1:16-17

YOU ARE A SON OF GOD. SONS ARE NOT REACTIONARY —they are governors of the unseen and seen realms. Everything in creation is subject to you. The systems of this world are not meant to dictate our reality—we were created to bring them into alignment.

We are co-heirs with Christ, meaning everything He governs, we govern with Him. The moment you shift from thinking as a servant to thinking as a son of God, everything changes. You stop chasing solutions and start commanding them.

The Kingdom is not coming—it is already here, within us. The only thing missing for it to be seen is manifested obedient sons who know who they are.

- Creation will not shift until we step into our divine identity.
- The remnant that gathers under the same spiritual vibration creates a supernatural synergy that accelerates heaven's manifestation.

Matthew 18:20 says, *"Where two or three are gathered in My name, I am there in the midst of them."* This coming together is not just about presence. Understand, our convergence is all about the governmental authority of God's kingdom being established in the earth. Through His sons. The more we embrace sonship, the more creation aligns, and the more the Kingdom is revealed in power.

When the remnant gathers under the same spiritual vibration (faith, glory, sonship), it creates a supernatural synergy that accelerates the release of heaven on earth. Jesus said, "Where two or three are gathered in My name, I am there in the midst of them." (Matthew 18:20). This is more than just presence—it speaks of governmental authority being established in the earth.

Note a few principles regarding Kingdom sonship:

- Sonship is a fundamental principle of royal representation.
- A son never lives for himself. A son is only on the earth to represent his Father.

- In the son the Father is glorified, and whatever the son does is only done when he hears his Father say, or he sees his Father do.
- That's the principle of sonship.
- Governing through sonship means ruling and stewarding the earth as mature sons and daughters (on Earth) of God, operating from identity.
- Sonship is about bringing Heaven's order into every sphere of society through wisdom, authority, and love.

ACCORDING TO THE ORIGINAL DESIGN, SONS DO NOT rule by striving. We rule by inheritance. God's intent was always for sons to govern the earth (Genesis 1:26).

Adam wasn't just given a job—he was given dominion as a son. Governance was not about control but about stewardship through relationship.

- Sons don't beg; they decree.
- Sons don't strive; they govern by nature.
- Dominion flows from identity, not effort.

When Adam fell, Sonship was lost—not religion.

That's why man replaced divine rulership with human systems of control, fear, and striving.

Remember: The Earth (Creation) responds to Sons, not slaves.

Creation was designed to recognize and respond to sons in authority (Romans 8:19). It doesn't respond to religion, titles, or effort—only to those who walk in true Sonship. When Adam and Eve sinned, they fell from dominion.

The ministry of the manifest Sons overturns the Adamic curse.

ELEVEN

WHEN WE FULLY EMBRACE OUR SONSHIP

WE CAN CHANGE THE WORLD

"For where two or three are gathered together in My name, I am there in the midst of them."

MATTHEW 18:20

WHEN JESUS SAID, "WHERE TWO OR THREE ARE gathered in My name, I am there in the midst of them," He released the intention of Father God, the King. This speaks of more than just presence—it speaks of governmental authority being established on Earth.

When the remnant gathers under the same spiritual vibration (faith, glory, sonship), it creates a supernatural synergy that accelerates the release of heaven on earth. The more we embrace sonship, the more creation aligns, and the more the Kingdom is revealed in governmental power.

IN OUR FINAL REVIEW, NOTE THESE THEOLOGICAL **truths about the Kingdom of God.**

The Kingdom of God is not just a future reality.

The Kingdom of God is an active, divine system that permeates and transforms both visible and invisible realms.

The Kingdom of God operates beyond human and satanic systems, enforcing God's sovereign will and eternal purposes in every realm.

The Kingdom of God does not just operate externally. It must first be established within the hearts of people.

This aligns with what Jesus emphasized when He said, in Luke 17:21: *"The Kingdom of God is within you."*

Kingdom gatherings are portals/doorways for Heaven's manifestation. A true Kingdom Gathering is not just a meeting—it is a spiritual portal where Heaven invades the earth, aligning frequencies, activating sonship, and releasing God's tangible presence.

When we learn to converge together in the Spirit, manifest from Sonship, and think from the eternal realm, we will see the Kingdom of God established in power.

Now is the time to step into your full identity, speak with authority, and align the world around you with the original blueprint of Heaven. Creation will not shift until we do.

CHAPTER ELEVEN

THE KINGDOM IS NOT COMING — IT IS HERE, WITHIN US. The only thing missing is manifested sons who know who they are.

TWELVE

ANSWERING THE GROANS OF CREATION

SONSHIP DECLARATIONS, & ACTIVATIONS

Day 1: The Son Awakens

Romans 8:19: *"For the earnest expectation of the creation eagerly waits for the revealing of the sons of God."*

Creation is not silent—it's groaning with the sound of expectation. Earth, its atmosphere, systems, even time itself are leaning forward in longing, waiting for me to emerge. I am not a spectator in this story. I am a son of God, the answer the earth is crying out for. There is an undeniable groan within—the sound of my spirit remembering something older than my body. Deep calls to the eternal something said—the truth of my origin in God, my assignment in Christ, and my calling as a manifested son.

Declaration: I am the sound that Creation has been waiting to hear. I awaken to my divine identity and purpose.

Activation: Where do I feel the "groan" in my life? How will I answer?

_____

_____

_____

Day 2: The True Image Of You

Genesis 1:26: *"Let Us make man in Our image, according to Our likeness..."*

I was not created to search for my image. I was created to carry the image of God's son. The image of Christ in me is not about appearance—it's about function, authority, and nature. To be made in His image is to be designed as a visible extension of an invisible reality. While the image was distorted by the fall in Eden, Jesus didn't come to tweak my humanity. He came to restore the blueprint for my life. And now, as a mature son, I move away from religion, for I am restored to my sonship image.

Declaration: The image of God in me is restored. I reflect His likeness with authority.

Activation: Ask the Holy Spirit, "What false images have I agreed with? Break agreement and write a new identity statement.

_____

_____

_____

_____

Day 3: From Teknon to Huios

Romans 8:14: *"As many as are led by the Spirit of God, these are sons (huios) of God."*

You may have started as a child (teknon), but Heaven sees a mature son (huios). Not just loved, but trusted. Not just born, but placed. The transition from teknon to huios is not about time— it's about yielding to the Spirit. Maturity is not measured in years, but in alignment. The huios are sons who carry the Father's heart. They don't beg for miracles, instead they embody the message. Mature sons do not visit God, we live and move in Him as His body.

Declaration: Today, my placement as a son is unveiled. I am not an orphan, I am a placed and trusted son. I walk in maturity and assignment.

Activation: Where is God calling me to rise from childlike dependency into son-level responsibility?

_____

_____

_____

_____

_____

Day 4: The Frequency of Glory

John 6:63: *"The words I speak to you are spirit and life."*

Everything God created responds to a frequency. The world was formed by His voice. His rhema doesn't just inform—it vibrates with creative force. As His son, you've been given the same access. When you speak from union in Him, your words create, align, and reform. Your voice is not just a sound—it is a signal to Creation. When you align with the Holy Spirit, your frequency changes—and everything around you begins to respond.

Declaration: I release Heaven's frequency with my voice. My words create, align, and bring Kingdom order into the Earth.

Activation: Make a point of intentionally changing an atmosphere. Speak a prophetic declaration over a space, situation, or person today. Release Heaven's creative frequencies.

_____

_____

_____

_____

_____

Day 5: Seated in Power

Ephesians 2:6: *"And raised us up together, and made us sit together in heavenly places in Christ Jesus..."*

Decree: You're not trying to get to Heaven—you're seated there now. This is more than positional theology, it is your functional authority. Sons legislate from the Throne room, not from the battlefield. God's seated sons release from a position of peace. You do not panic, you rule from seated rest. When your spirit is seated, your soul aligns. As your soul aligns, your body manifests dominion.

Declaration: I am seated with Christ. I legislate from rest. I rule with authority.

Activation: Ask: What area of my life am I striving in that I should be seated in? Surrender it.

_____

_____

_____

_____

_____

Day 6: Sonship Unveiled

2 Corinthians 3:18: *"We all, with unveiled face, beholding the glory... are being transformed into the same image..."*

Decree: You are not hiding anymore. The veil is lifting, revealing the true, eternal you. As you behold Him, you don't just see Jesus—you start seeing your reflection in Him. You're not separated. You're not incomplete. You are being transfigured into the image you were always meant to carry. And the world is also beginning to see it.

Declaration: As I behold Him, I am unveiled and transformed by His glory.

Activation: Stand before a mirror. Prophesy over your own reflection with unveiled truth, according to the Word of God.

_____

_____

_____

_____

_____

_____

Day 7: The Reformer Within

Romans 8:21: *"Creation itself will be delivered into the glorious liberty of the children of God."*

You are not waiting for revival—you are the reformation. Creation responds to sons who know their assignment, walk in alignment, and release the frequency of Eden into systems, structures, and nations. You are not here to escape. You are here to restore. You are the first fruit of the new creation —proof that union has been restored, dominion returned, and Eden is near.

Declaration: I am a reformer. I restore order, identity, and glory to creation.

Activation: Write out what area of culture (family, education, media, government, etc.) you are called to reform.

_____

_____

_____

_____

_____

_____

"THE LORD BLESS YOU AND KEEP YOU; THE LORD MAKE HIS FACE SHINE UPON YOU, AND BE GRACIOUS TO YOU; THE LORD LIFT UP HIS COUNTENANCE UPON YOU, AND GIVE YOU PEACE."

NUMBERS 6:24-26

ABOUT THE AUTHOR

Dr. Marshall McGee is an internationally recognized apostolic and prophetic leader whose ministry has transformed lives for over 50 years. As the founder of Kingdom Mandate Fellowship Global and co-founder of Agape Worship Center International, he equips leaders to discover their divine assignment and walk in Kingdom authority with clarity and power.

Known for his wisdom, humor, and revelatory insight, Dr. McGee has ministered in over 20 nations, raising up spiritual sons and daughters and releasing many into prophetic and five-fold ministry. His message is simple but profound: Learn to *Live full. Die empty.*

A dynamic communicator and mentor, his ministry is marked by healing, deliverance, and powerful demonstrations of the Holy Spirit. He is also a certified life coach, a police chaplain with the Omaha Police Department, and the host of the weekly television program "Kingdom Perspectives" on Kingdom First TV.

Dr. McGee holds advanced degrees in leadership and theology and continues to serve as a trusted voice to churches, leaders, and reformers across the globe. He and his wife, Prophet Randi McGee, reside in Omaha, Nebraska, where their ministry headquarters serves as a hub for Kingdom advancement and global impact.

You can learn more about their ministry at www.kmfglobal.org.